A Different Kind of Boy

A story about inclusion and making friends

by Michael Simones

Illustrated by Eminence System

This book may be purchased by contacting the publisher and author (wcrowspub@gmail.com).

Publisher: White Crow S-Publishing

ISBN-979-8-9877310-0-0 (softcover)
ISBN-979-8-9877310-1-7 (hardcover)
Library of Congress Control Number: 2023917519

Printed in the U.S.A

Dedication

I recognize the daily guidance of God in my life and I am so grateful for it. Without God I would have achieved nothing in this life. I thank God for guiding me to a career of promoting inclusion and affirming support for all types of children.

A Note for
Parents and Teachers

Around the ages of 5-7 (the early school-age years), children begin to develop a sense of who they are. This internal development is influenced by external experiences and messages, both negative and positive, about who they are as an individual, and this can impact on a child's self esteem.

Affirming messages of inclusion for *all* are essential in life, whether at home, in the classroom or–perhaps especially–on the playground. It is for this reason that I wrote this book.

Michael Simones

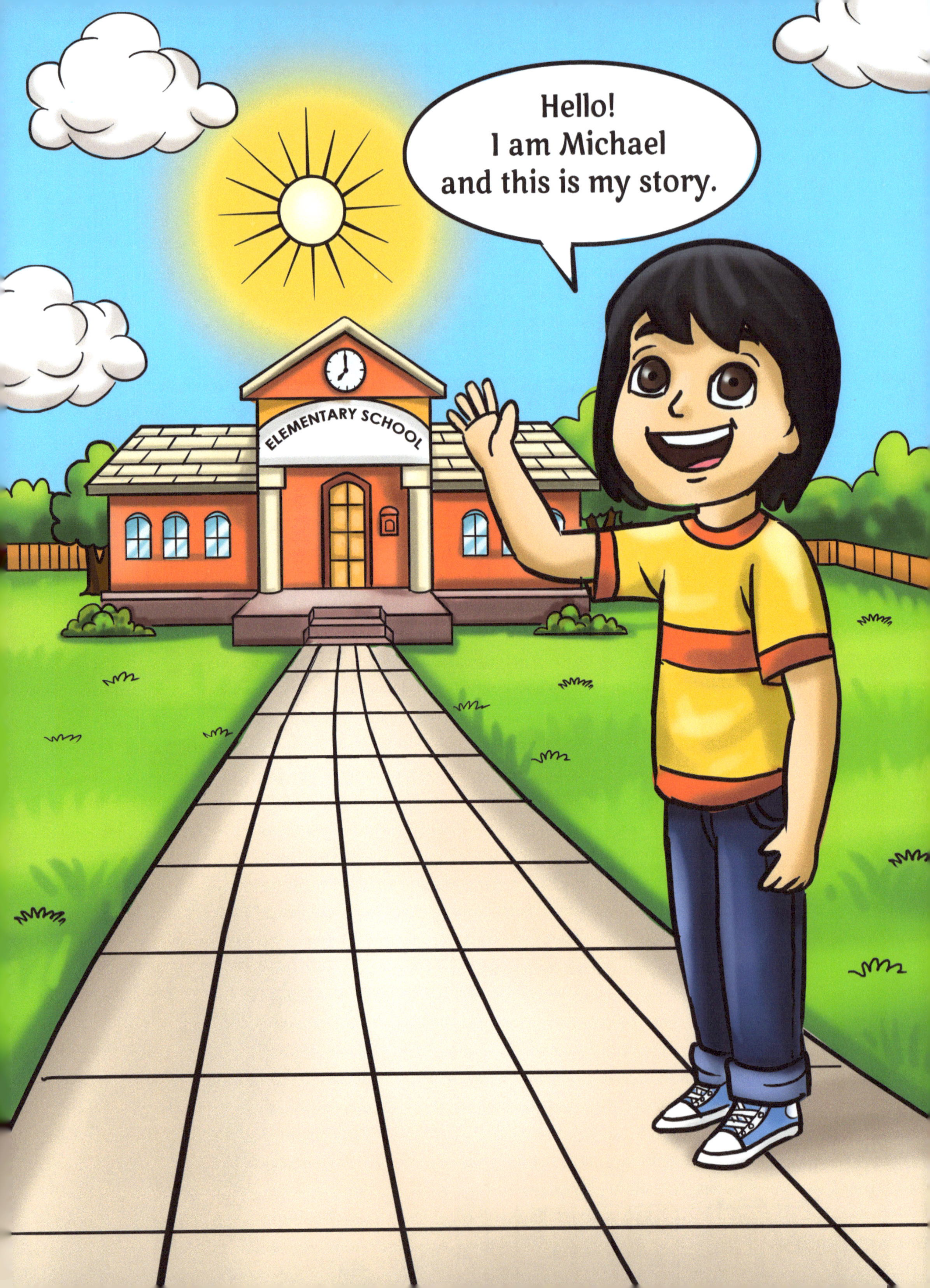
Hello!
I am Michael
and this is my story.
ELEMENTARY SCHOOL

Chapters

Chapter 1: Different

Hi, I'm Michael! I feel different, but in a good way.

Other boys my age like playing ball, racing cars, wrestling with each other, and getting messy and dirty.

I don't like those things, so at first, it was hard for me to make friends with other boys. They teased me for not liking the things they like. They called me names, and sometimes they even pushed me over and hit me.

I liked my friends that were girls. I could be myself with them. But I wished I could find a friend who was a boy, so that I could have both boys and girls as friends.

Chapter 2: Lance & Jim

Two boys, called Lance and Jim, bullied me because I don't like the things the other boys like. They wanted to make me feel bad about being different.

Lance called me names like "Sissy" and "Fairy," and he looked at me like I was a freak.

Jim liked to pretend to hit me; sometimes he hit me for real.

I got scared when I saw them, but I also wished I could be tough like them.

But, I didn't want to be mean like them.

My friends that are girls stuck up for me and tried to protect me from Lance and Jim. It worked most of the time...but not all of the time.

I tried to talk with Lance and Jim hoping I can stop the bullying, but nothing I did changed their minds about me. And all because I don't like playing ball.

Chapter 3: Playing Ball

To me, playing ball is not fun! I don't like rolling around the grass or in the dirt. I don't like all the yelling and being hit by the ball. It's just not fun for me!

What I *do* like is reading books, swimming, and learning all kinds of science. Oh–and I'm crazy about vampire stories!

These things are quite different to playing ball, so boys like Lance and Jim think it's okay to make fun me, and even hurt me.

For some reason, playing ball seems important to boys. I don't understand why!

But I'm not the only boy who feels this way…

Chapter 4: Bruce & Andy

There are two other boys in my class who don't like playing ball or getting dirty in the grass or dirt. Their names are Bruce and Andy.

Bruce is one of the smartest kids in our class. He always finishes his assignments first, and has no problem solving math problems—my worst subject! Bruce is very quiet. He is nice to everyone and very helpful! He gets bullied too, but not as much as me. I think it was because he's so quiet.

Bruce dresses more formal than the rest of us. Kind of like he's going to church in his Sunday best. The clothes he wears to school aren't meant for rough play, and I never see him playing ball. During recess he likes to sit somewhere shaded, and read. We have two things in common—so I thought he might be a good friend for me!

If there was anyone who got bullied more than me, it was Andy, a new kid who had recently moved here.

At recess I saw Andy hanging out with his older sister at the monkey bars. Since he was new, I didn't know what things he liked to do. But I thought that if we became friends, I could find out! I did know that I never saw him playing ball.

Andy was teased and bullied by Lance and Jim, mostly because of his appearance. He's kind of frumpy and awkward. He wears baggy clothes and shoes a size or two too big for him. Nobody seems to care about that except Lance and Jim. Oh boy— Lance and Jim just don't like anyone who's different!

I thought I could use a friend, and I knew Andy could too! The right and smart thing to do would be to try and make friends with both Bruce and Andy. Then I would have both boys and girls as friends!

But instead of trying to become friends with Bruce and Andy, I did something bad...

Chapter 5: Michael the Bully

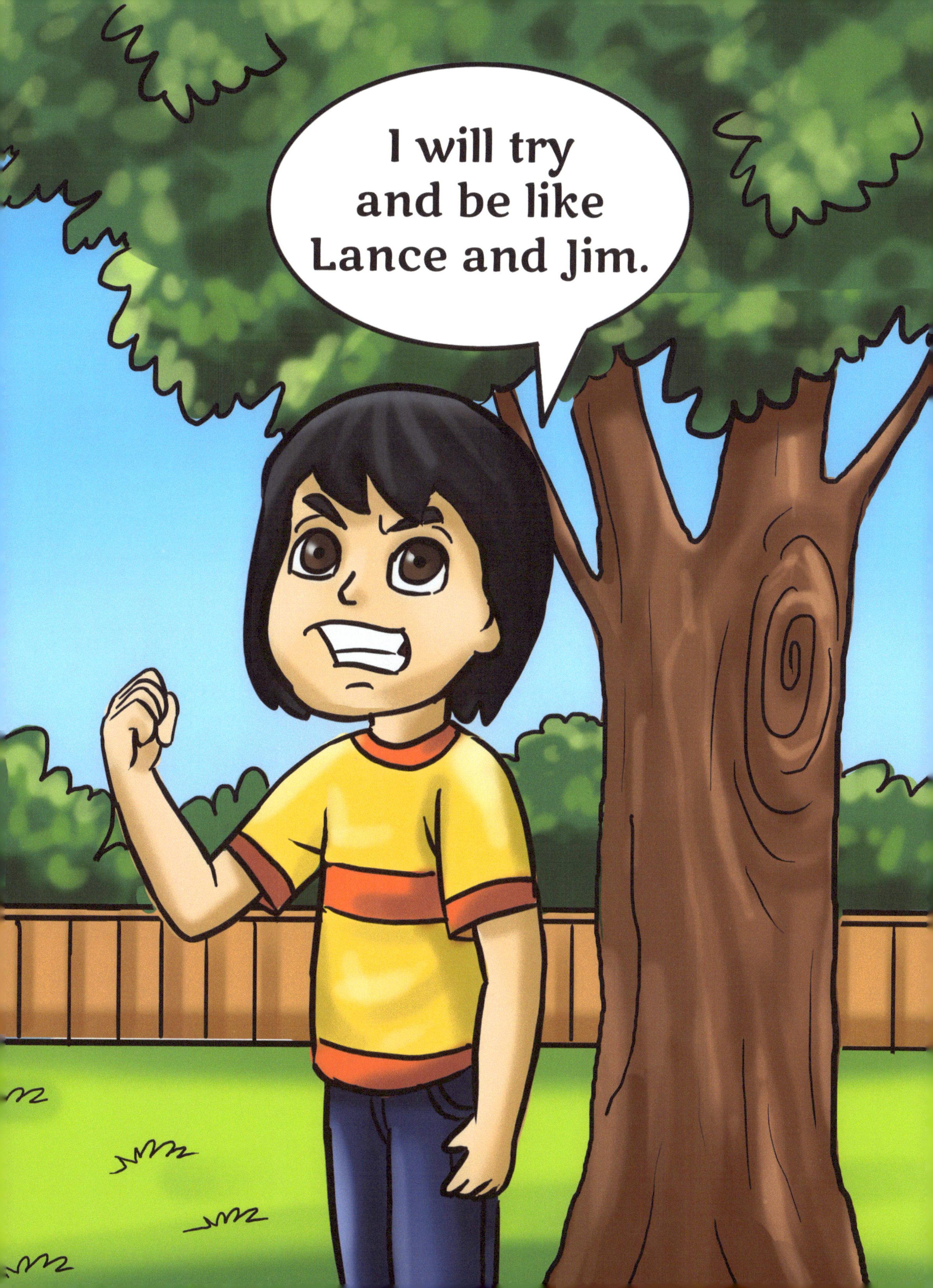
I will try and be like Lance and Jim.

I was the opposite to friendly. I began to bully them too!

I was trying to feel better about myself, and be like Lance and Jim. I thought that maybe if I became a bully like them, they would accept me and stop picking on me.

Boy—was I wrong!

I bullied Bruce for being so dressed up at school. I picked on Andy for his baggy clothes.

Then, one day, I got what I deserved. Bruce had enough of me and pushed me down to the ground, yelling, "I hate you!"

I felt so bad inside. I didn't want to be bad anymore. Being like Lance and Jim only hurts good kids!

Chapter 6: Michael the Friend

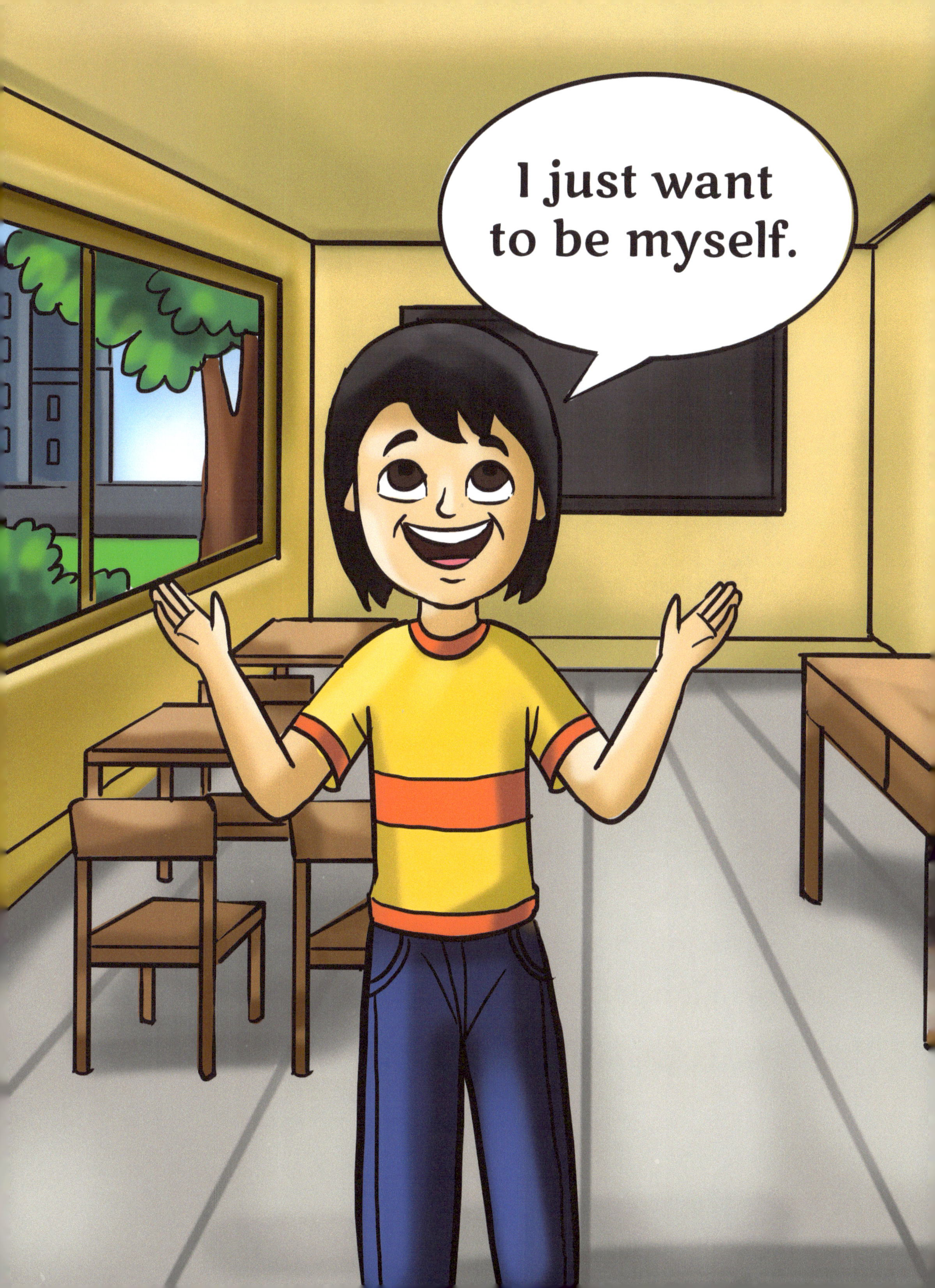
I just want to be myself.

The first thing I did was say sorry to Bruce. I told him the truth—that what I really wanted was to be his friend.

I asked Bruce if he would help me pick out some good books at the library. He said, "Okay!" After the trip to the library, we read and shared books together almost everyday.

When we weren't reading books we played by the monkey bars with Andy. We found out that the three of us like scary things, and that's what made us friends.

Andy likes monster toys, Bruce likes ghost stories and, as you know, I like vampire stories. Andy started bringing his monster toys to school to show us (our teacher hated that) and Bruce and I shared monster, ghost and vampire books.

That's when Andy started reading with us!

WE BECAME GREAT FRIENDS!

Chapter 7: Lessons I Learned

The lessons I learned are:

When you are different, try to find friends like you!

Don't let bullies get you down!

Don't become a bully! When you are a bully you miss out on getting to know great kids like Bruce and Andy!

ALWAYS REMEMBER TO BE YOURSELF!

www.ingramcontent.com/pod-product-compliance
Lightning Source LLC
Chambersburg PA
CBHW042123040426
42450CB00002B/49